White Witching

  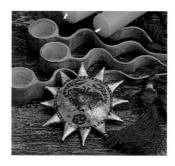

Co

Mariano Kälfors

White
Witching

The good magic-maker's guide
to spellweaving

LORENZ BOOKS

This e

Lorenz
Herme
tel. 020
www.lo
info@a

© Anne

Publish
27 Wes
fax 212

Publish
Level 1
tel. (02)

This ed
tel. 020

This ed
tel. 301

This ed
tel. 416

This ed
tel. (09)

A CIP o

Publishe
Manag
Art Ma
Consult

1 0 9 8

Severa
Spellwe

Introduction

Today, ordinary people from all walks of life are practising witches. From the woman next door to the high-flying business executive, there are as many practising witches as there ever have been. These modern-day witches should not be confused with the ones who gave witchcraft a bad name. If you meet a witch it is much more likely to be a "white" one who uses the powers of magic for good, weaving spells to bring greater prosperity, health, happiness and wellbeing.

witches and spells

So what is a witch exactly? Some people think the word "witch" comes from an Old English word meaning "to know" but others say that it means "to cast a spell". A modern witch can be male or female, and you could say that it is someone who uses their "knowing" to bring about a desired result through the weaving of spells.

...being a witch today is not as outlandish as it may seem...

A spell is like a special recipe, uniquely designed to initiate a chain of events so as to make your wish come true. When a spell is cast, it is the intention and concentration of the spell-weaver that gives the spell its power. White witches only ever make spells that have a positive intention, and never ever seek to harm or cause pain to another. They believe in the "law of three": that what you put out will return threefold – so it makes good sense to only work with positive, loving energies as these are what will come back.

becoming a white witch

With patience and practice, anyone can be a white witch. It's about developing a relationship with the natural world and using magic to help yourself and others. You can work magic to gain more control over your life – to start making it go the way you want, rather than leaving things to chance. You can use it for healing, to create opportunities, or to foster friend-ships. Use it for anything you want – so long as it harms no one.

Above Anyone can be a witch today and many practising are about as ordinary looking as the girl next door.

Left A mirror symbolizes psychic powers and is a common tool used by witches for divination.

The basics

Before you start flicking the pages and looking for the spells, there are a few things you should know first about white witchcraft in general, and about how to prepare yourself for spellweaving.

...what every self-respecting witch needs to know...

This section will give you a good grounding of the rudimentary basics. The first few pages will provide an informative insight into what witches believe. You will learn about the witch's belief in the power of nature and our links with the cosmos, and how the changing seasons of the year and the patterns of the stars and planets influence our life on earth. The traditions behind the witch's

annual festivals are explained, and how to work with the powers of the moon, the sun and the four elements throughout the year. You will also learn useful and

...the power of nature and our links with the cosmos...

practical information about the witch's tool kit, where and when it is best to spellweave, and

about the preparation rituals that you need to follow prior to working a spell. And lastly, don't miss the special pages on meditation, scrying and inner journeys; all very useful further knowledge to help you on your path to practising white witchcraft.

The spells

This is where the magic really starts. This section contains more than thirty spells to bring a little sparkle into all areas of your life. The spells begin with meeting celestial angels and personal guides and

then you can start to work magic for healing and protection, self-empowerment, luck and prosperity, love and romance, friends and relationships, and much more.

Working with a variety of magical ingredients, including talismans, amulets, charms, spellbags and an assortment of

...to be good of heart is the true key to real magic...

stones, plants, herbs, trees and oils, you can begin to spellweave. Find out how to increase your aura of self-confidence, remove obstacles,

...the spells that follow are spells of beauty and power...

improve your day-to-day business and other affairs, enhance your career prospects, ensure safe travel, or attract the perfect mate. You can also clear negative vibes, find your direction in life and

learn how to boost a flagging self-esteem.

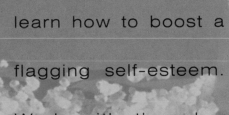

Work with the phases of the moon to increase your psychic powers and strengthen your spellmaking abilities, and use the power of the sun for health, success and prosperity.

Increasing abundance

There's no virtue in being poor. We live on a rich and fertile planet so it makes sense to share in nature's bounty. But in order for prosperity to come to you, you need first to give freely of yourself.

you will need
- 2.7m (9ft) white cord
- four pinches of tobacco
- gold candle
- blessed silver coin
- 15cm (6in) square of orange silk
- fresh spearmint leaves
- orange thread

best time
- Sunday
- waxing moon

preparation
Carry the coin with you for seven days from Sunday to Sunday. During the week, give something of yourself for free that costs time and energy, such as cleaning for a friend.

1 Open your circle in the east and make offerings of tobacco to each of the four directions. Stand in the centre of the circle and light the candle.

2 Take out your silver coin and hold it in the palm of your left hand. Hold the gold candle in the other hand and face south. Say the invocation, passing your coin through the flame of the candle six times:

O Angel Michael, I ask you to help me to understand the nature of abundance, that I may become wealthy in spirit, as well as in affluence. I ask you to bring me the riches that I need in order to live comfortably. I ask for the right amount of prosperity to fill my life that will meet my needs and so give the time and energy to use my gifts, to celebrate life and to help others in poverty or unhappiness. Grant me this and I will remember to give as I have received.

3 Say "thank you" after the request, and place the coin in the orange silk square with some spearmint leaves, and bind with orange thread. Carry this with you in your coin purse, or keep it in a tin box at home or somewhere else where it will be safe.

4 Moving widdershins from the north, gather up the tobacco, saying "thank you" to each of the four directions as you do so. When you have finished closing say "and so may it be" and visualize the spell being carried into the universe.

5 Give the tobacco back to the earth by placing it underneath a tree – preferably an almond, horse chestnut, oak or field maple.

Right Even witches like to live in abundance and have to make some effort towards prosperity!

Work with tree magic for a good luck spell. Perform this whenever you are leaving something behind and starting something new. This can be anything from taking exams or starting college, to a new job or moving house.

you will need
- small amethyst
- turquoise stone
- oak leaves
- cinquefoil essential oil
- sprig of rosemary
- spellbag

best time
- Thursday
- full moon

preparation
Find a suitable spellbag (a small drawstring pouch). Look in any New Age shop or stores selling hand-crafted goods, or even make your own. This spell is performed at an oak tree, so find a suitable one in your area.

1 Greet your oak tree and tell it your intentions. Place the small amethyst at its base as an offering. Walking deosil in a circle, repeat four times:

O Sachiel, Angel of Jupiter, I ask you to hear my call. Light my path, guide my actions, words and thoughts and those of all I am yet to meet, that by the power of your might, all will be fortunate to my sight.

Good fortune growing, growing, growing, growing.

2 Anoint the turquoise stone and leaves with cinquefoil oil, while visualizing yourself surrounded by the arms of the mighty oak tree.

3 Place the anointed turquoise stone, the sprig of rosemary and the oak leaves in your spellbag. Hold it up to the oak tree and say out loud:

Heart of Oak, you are my heart and with honour I shall carry you by my side.

Thank you.

Right The oak tree lives for hundreds of years and is a symbol of strength. It grants good fortune to all who seek its blessings and is also a guardian tree, offering protection and courage.

4 Carry your spell with you at all times when you are seeking good fortune, and store it carefully when not in use. You could also do this spell as a special gift for a friend, using their name in place of yours throughout.

amethyst

Generally a healing stone, amethyst is also very good for calming the mind and helping with meditation. As you use the stone you may become aware of an increased imagination and ability to visualize clearly.

Drawing down the moon

The moon is the protector and guardian of women. Draw on her powers to refresh and rejuvenate you for the month ahead, or if you are a man, to help you get more in touch with your sensitivity and powers of intuition.

you will need
- 13 circular stones, river stones or crystals
- salt
- aromatherapy burner
- jasmine essential oil
- 9 white or cream candles

best time
- up to two days before full moon

1 Beginning in the south, lay down 12 of your chosen stones in a deosil direction (it doesn't matter whether or not the stones are the same size as one another). Place the 13th stone in the centre.

2 Sprinkle the stones with a little salt. Light the burner and put in three drops of jasmine oil.

3 Place eight candles around the circle, and one by the centre stone. As you light the candles say:

Magna Dea, Light of the Night, I light these candles to guide your moonrays here. I ask you to come and bless this circle.

4 Facing south, stand with your arms outstretched above your head and your feet quite wide apart. Reach towards the sky. Say the lunar invocation:

Hail to thee, Sophia, holy spirit of the wise moon. I call upon you to enter and fill me with your light. Protect me and guide me on the moonway. Teach me your wisdom and truth as I seek your clarity and guidance.

5 Imagine drawing down the powers of the moon into yourself. Allow yourself to be refreshed and refilled with the feminine virtues of wisdom, beauty and grace. Let the moon bless your feelings and perceptions until you feel energized and content. Bring your arms down to your sides.

6 Close your circle widdershins, saying "thank you" as you blow out the candles. Dispose of any organic ingredients in a safe place outside.

Below Both men and women are intimately linked to the changing faces of the moon as it progresses through its cycle.

Lunar wishes

A talisman is a written wish and can take any form. Make a lunar talisman to draw on the powers of the moon. Remember: a new to full moon is the time for drawing things to you; a full to dark moon is the time for letting go.

you will need

- wand
- 2 silver or white candles
- moonstone
- silver pen
- ruler
- 23cm (9in) square of natural paper

best time

- Monday
- time your spell according to the correct moon phase for attracting or releasing something.

1 Open a sacred circle and put your spell ingredients in the centre. Facing north, light the candles, saying as you do so:

Hail to you Levanah, I light these candles in your honour and ask for your assistance this night.

2 Translate your first name into numbers using the chart below. For example the name Isabel becomes 911253. Then work out the sigil for your name by tracing the shape of those numbers on the Kamea of the Moon. Draw a 5cm (2in) square in the top left-hand corner of the paper with the silver pen and copy your sigil into it. Write your wish in the remaining space.

1	2	3	4	5	6	7	8	9
A	B	C	D	E	F	G	H	I
J	K	L	M	N	O	P	Q	R
S	T	U	V	W	X	Y	Z	

3 Fold the four corners of the paper into the centre, then repeat twice more.

4 Hold the moonstone next to your stomach and silently ask:

Levanah, I offer this moonstone in your honour, and ask that you imbue it with your power to make my wish come true.

5 When you have finished, say "thank you" and close the circle in the usual way. If your talisman is for an "attracting something to you" wish, leave it, together with the moonstone, in the light of the increasing moon until your wish is granted. If it is for a "letting go of something" wish, take the talisman and stone to a river or seashore on the first night after full moon and place it in the water to be taken away. Watch it leave, and then turn away. Do not look back.

kamea of the moon

In magic, the moon is associated with the number nine. Use its powers to create a special moon talisman for enhancing perception and increasing psychic powers. The sigil for Isabel has been added as an example. The sigil should always begin as a circle and end in a line.

37	78	29	70	21	62	13	54	5
6	38	79	30	71	22	63	14	46
47	7	39	80	31	72	23	55	15
16	48	8	40	81	32	64	24	56
57	17	48	⑨	41	73	33	65	25
26	58	18	50	1	42	74	34	66
67	27	59	10	51	2	43	75	35
36	68	19	60	11	52	3	44	76
77	28	69	20	61	12	53	4	45

If you feel you are hiding your light or that others simply don't notice you, it's easy to become discouraged. Work with the powers of the moon to bring yourself out of the darkness and receive the recognition you deserve.

you will need
- silver altar cloth
- 3 silver or white candles
- natural paper
- silver pen
- envelope
- silver or glass bowl of spring water

best time
- full moon

preparation
This spell uses an altar. In the evening when the moon has risen, prepare your altar by blessing and laying out your equipment. Arrange the candles in a crescent shape to symbolize the moon.

1 Light the three candles from left to right saying:

Moon Maiden inspire me, Moon Mother protect me, Moon Matriarch empower me, as I ask this favour. At this hour of bright moonlight, please help me to shine at what I do, and to receive fitting reward for my efforts.

2 Close your eyes and really focus on what it is you need and are trying to achieve; this could be a promotion at work, or a pay rise, or simply for your friends to take more notice of you. Take the silver pen and write out your exact and precise need.

3 Fold the paper and put it in the envelope and seal it carefully. Hold the envelope below each candle in turn, so that the light of the candle shines on it. Be careful not to let the paper singe or burn.

4 Sprinkle the envelope with water in front of each of the three candles from left to right in turn, saying:

Moon Maiden bless me, Moon Mother guide me and Moon Matriarch assist me that my will be done.

5 Blow out the candles from left to right, giving thanks to each aspect of the moon in turn.

6 Hide the envelope away until the next full moon. You may be surprised at the results. If it is a particularly persistent problem, you may need to keep working with this spell every month at full moon.

Below As this is a moon ritual, you need to set out your altar accordingly with white and silver items to represent her.

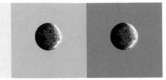

Opening the inner gates

The gate of inner vision, or the "third eye", is situated on the forehead just above the eyebrows. When this gate is open, it gives you access to inner vision and enhanced psychic power.

you will need
- 2.7m (9ft) white cord
- flower
- red candle
- small bowl of water
- stone
- sandalwood incense
- a picture of an open door or gate

best time
- Monday
- waxing moon

1 Open your cord circle and place the flower in the east, the candle in the south, the bowl of water in the west and the stone in the north. Light the incense in the centre of the circle.

2 Sit in the centre with the picture of the open door or gate on your lap. Close your eyes, centre yourself and focus on your intention: be sure that your wish to work with inner vision is for the highest good of all.

3 Stand up and make opening gestures to each of the four quarters. Say the following as you pick up each object:

*Open my mind like a growing flower,
may my vision now empower,*

*Open my mind to the candle fire,
may my vision now inspire,* [light the candle]

Open my mind to the water's flow, that on vision journeys I may go

Open my mind to this stone so cold, that visions I shall safely hold.

Right Use the power of the light of the moon to enhance your psychic ability and inner vision.

4 Pick up the open gate or door picture and hold it out in front of your heart. Circle or turn around four times saying:

Open gates that I may roam

Safely bring my knowledge home.

5 Sit down and close your eyes again. Relax and sit in meditation for a while, letting any pictures or images come and go. When you are ready, open your eyes and put out the incense, and close the circle widdershins.

6 Keep a record of what you have experienced in words and/or pictures.

Index

Acknowledgements

Photography by Peter
Anderson, Simon Bottomley,
Jonathan Buckley, John
Freeman, Michelle Garrett,
Don Last, William Lingwood,
Gloria Nicol, Debbie Patterson,
Fiona Pragoff, Peter Williams
and Polly Wreford.